HUMAN ORGANS, WHAT & WHY? THIRD GRADE SCIENCE TEXTBOOK SERIES

Speedy Publishing LLC
40 E. Main St. #1156
Newark, DE 19711
www.speedypublishing.com

Copyright 2018

An organ is a collection of tissues joined in a structural unit to serve a common function.

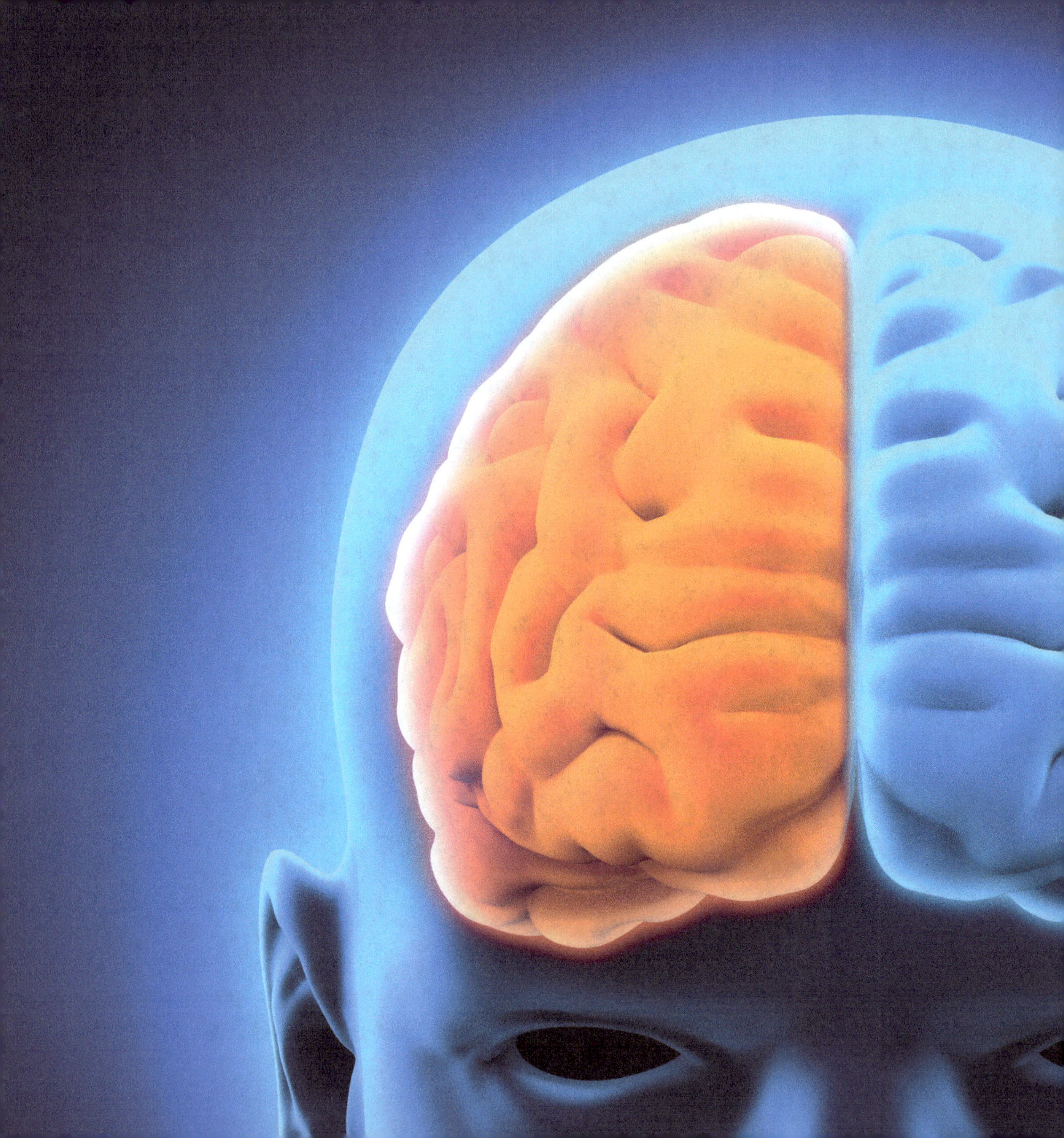

Perhaps the most important organ in our body is the brain. The brain is an organ that serves as the center of the nervous system.

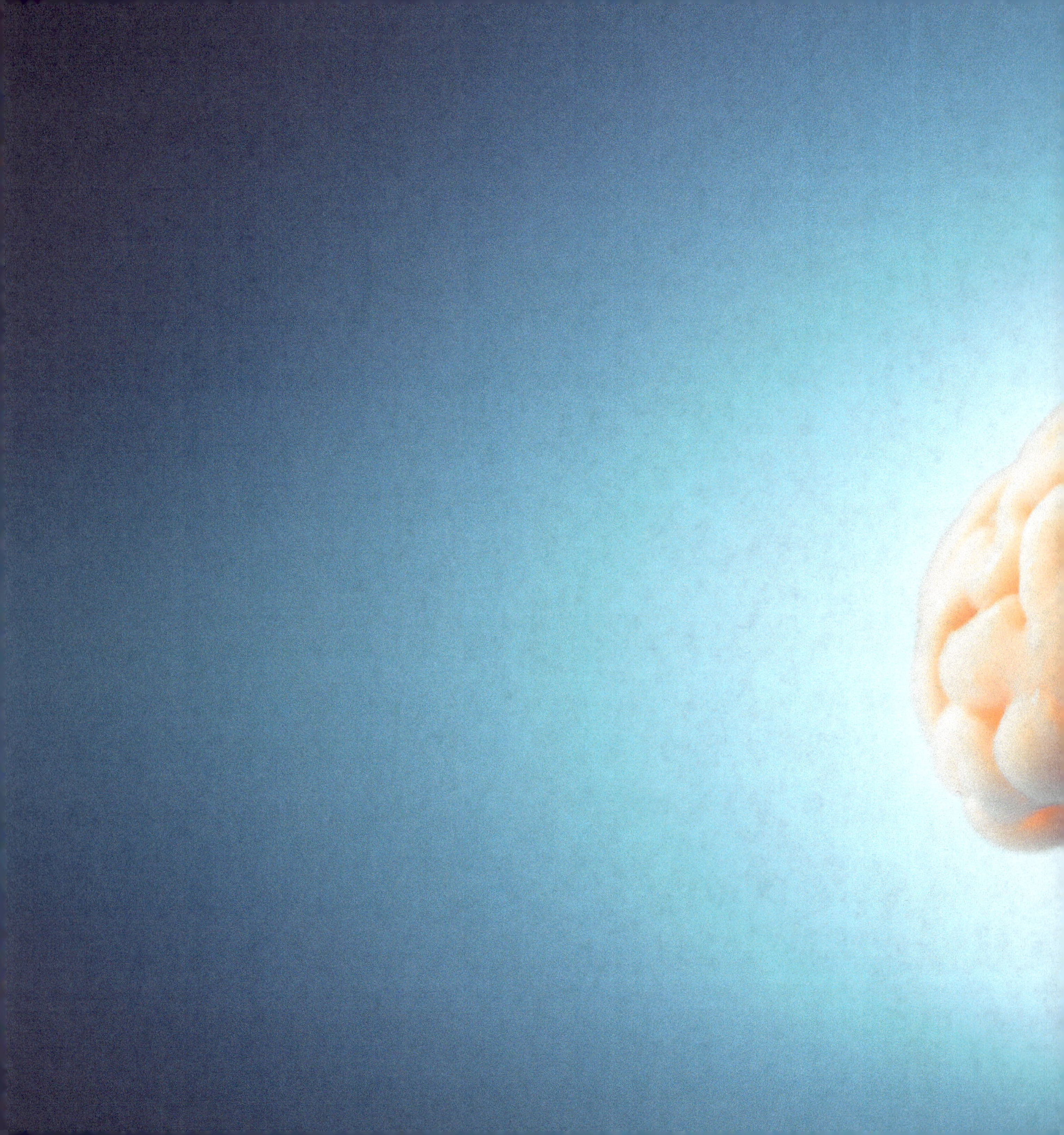

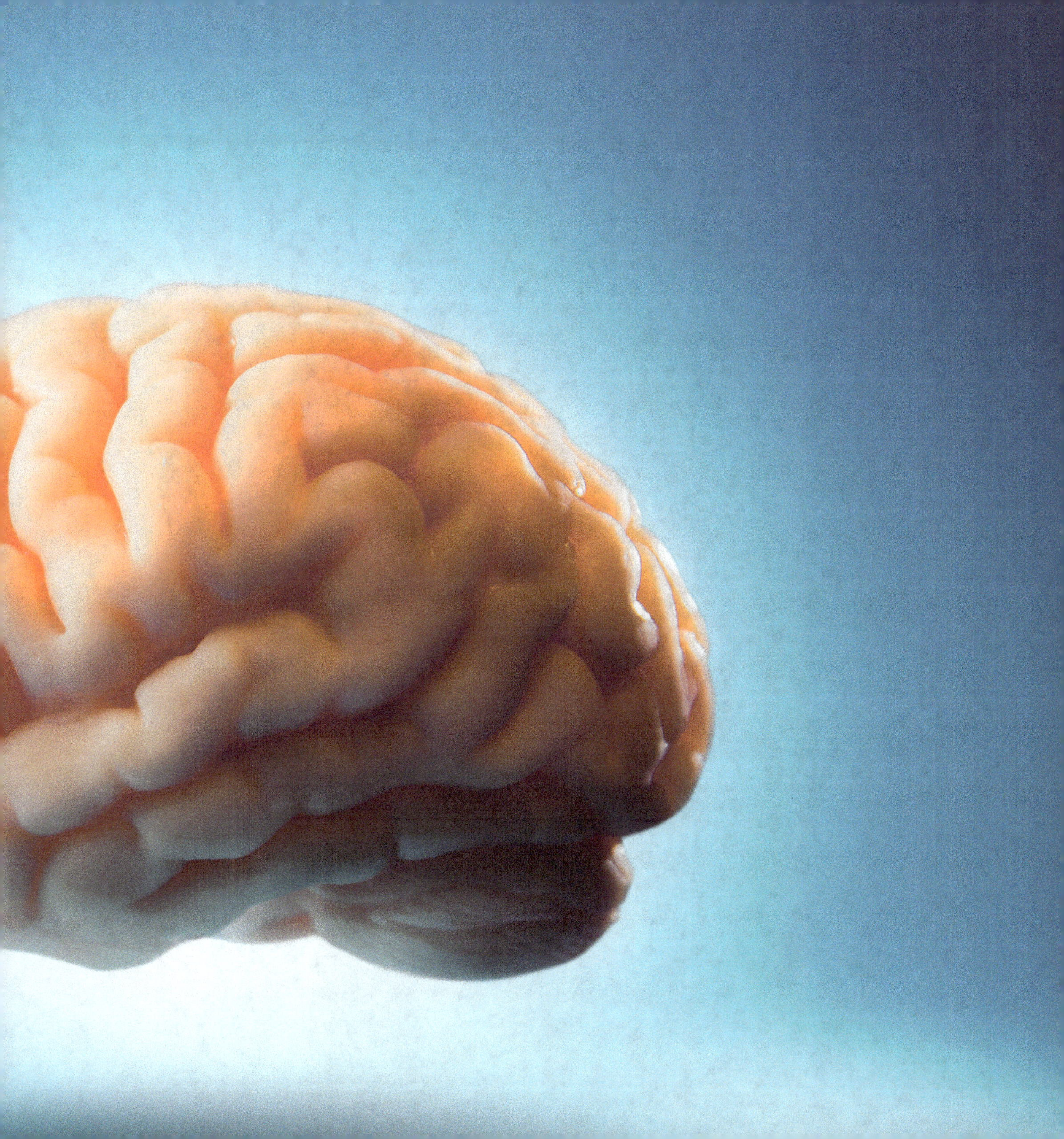

Lungs are major organs that bring much needed oxygen into our blood stream and release carbon dioxide from the bloodstream into the atmosphere.

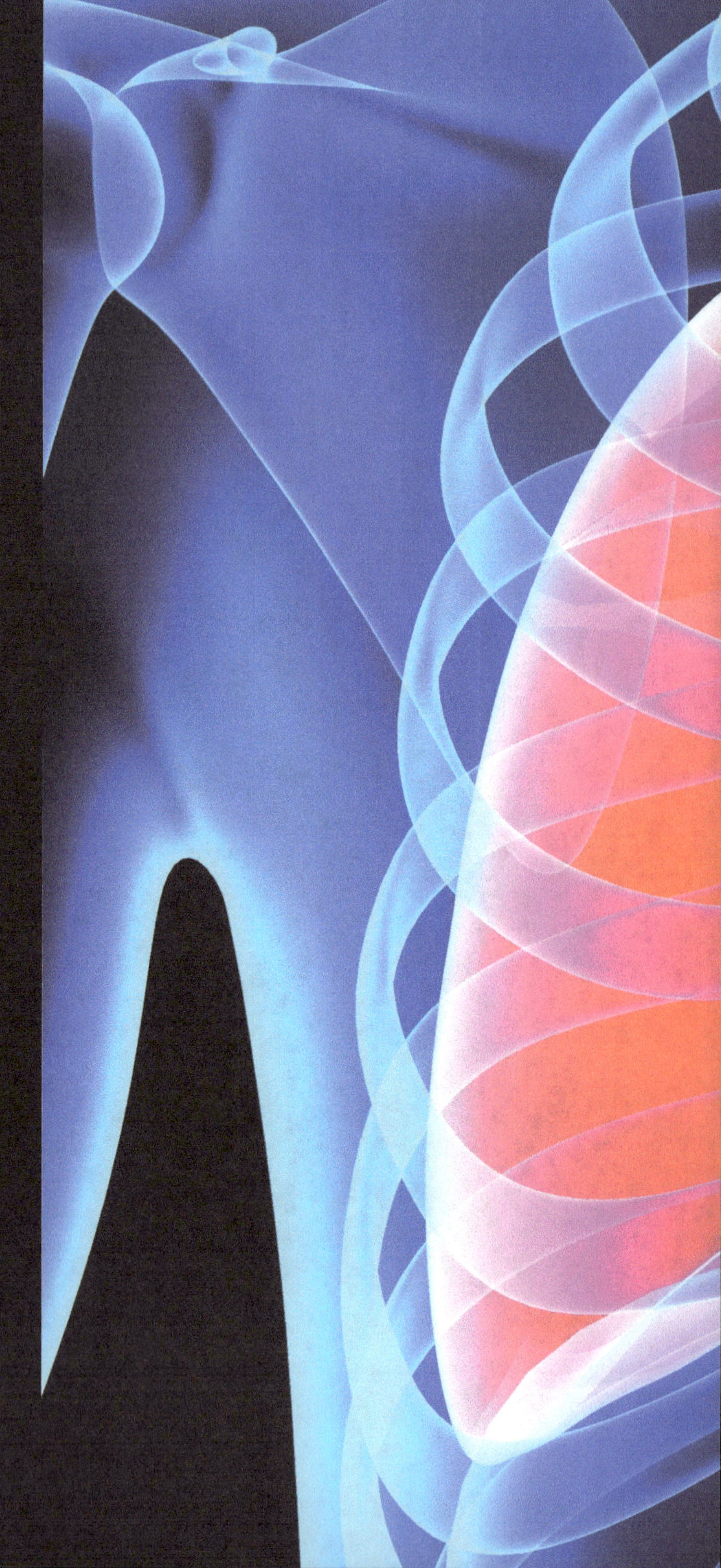

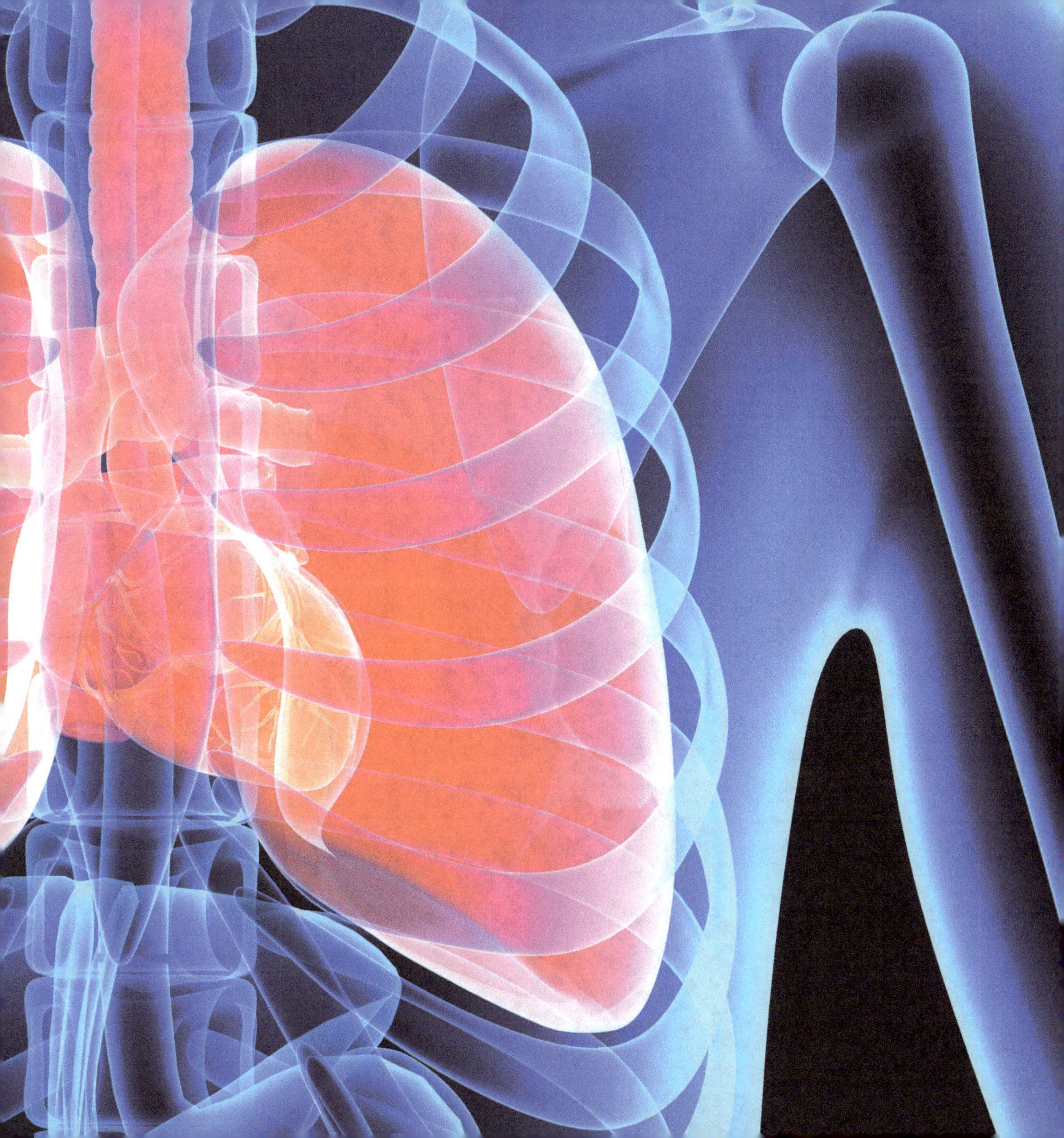

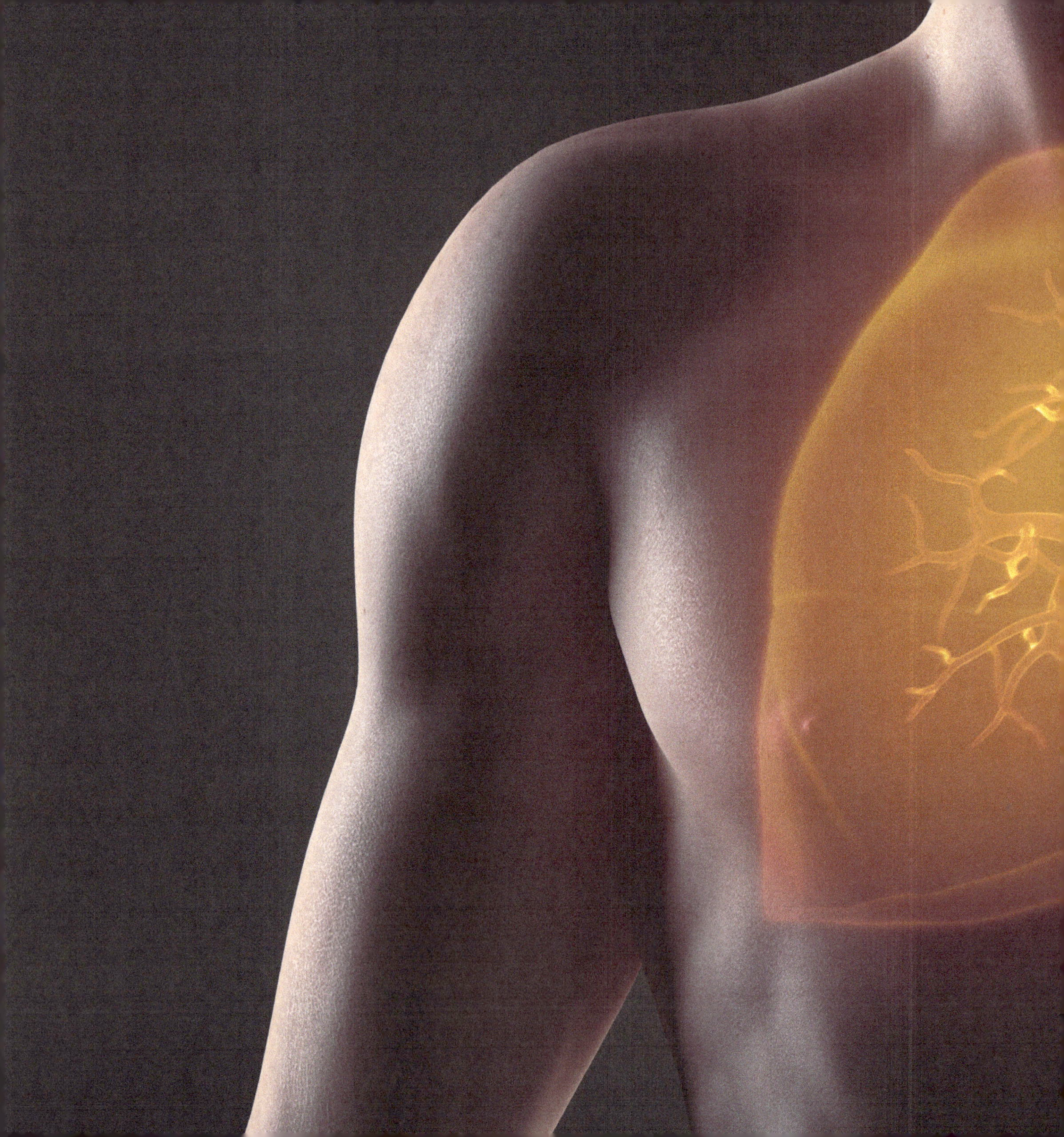

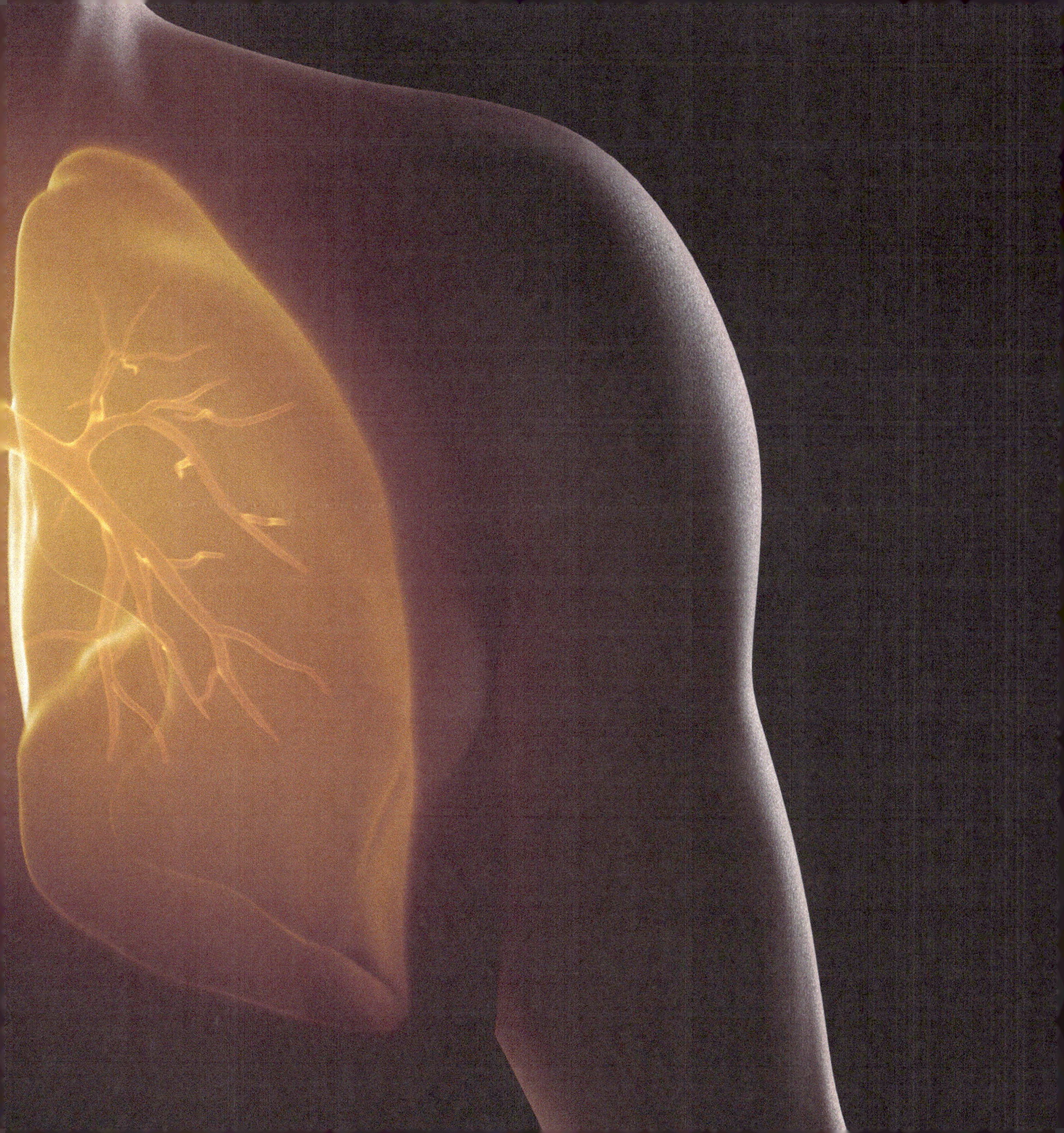

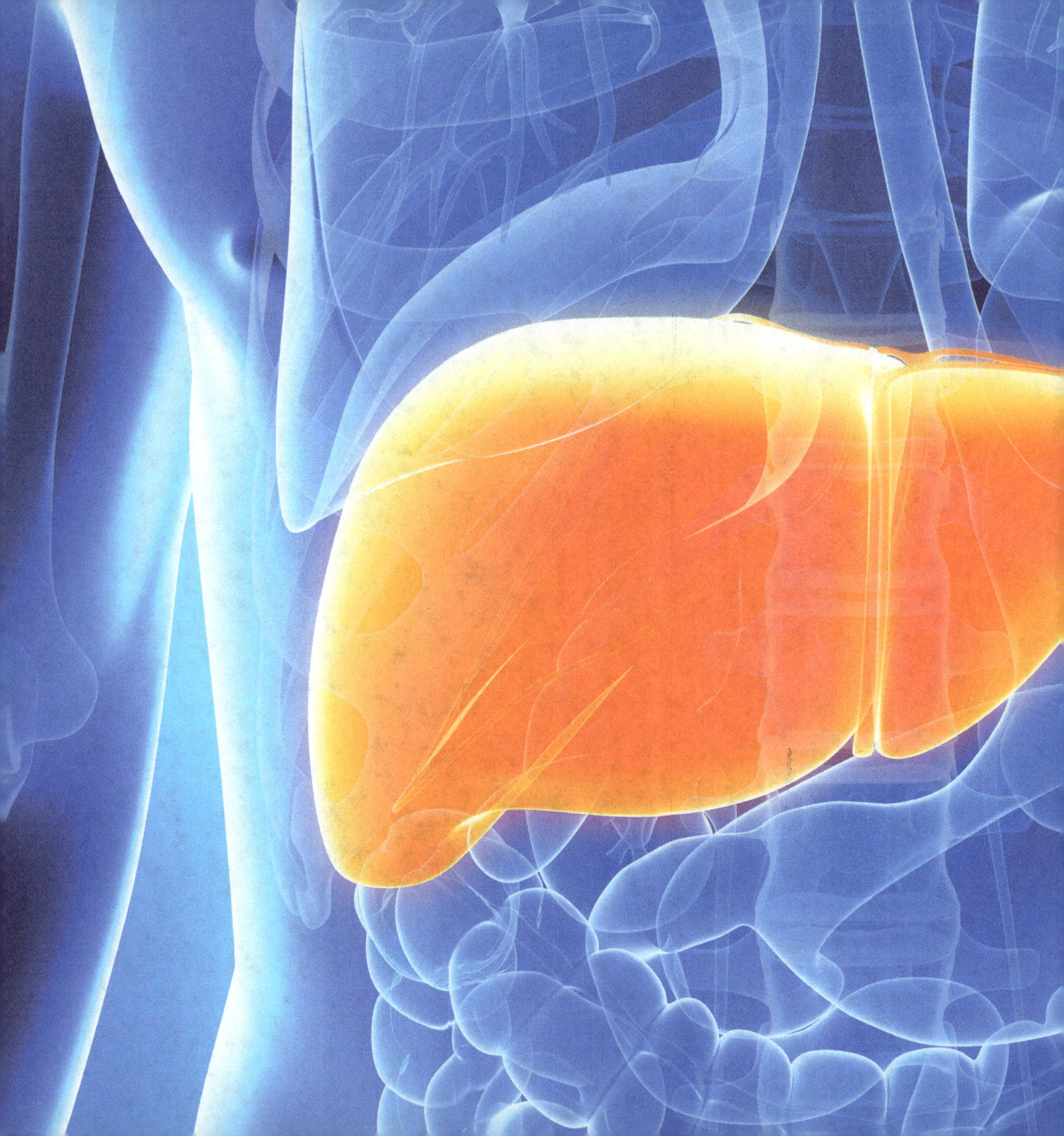

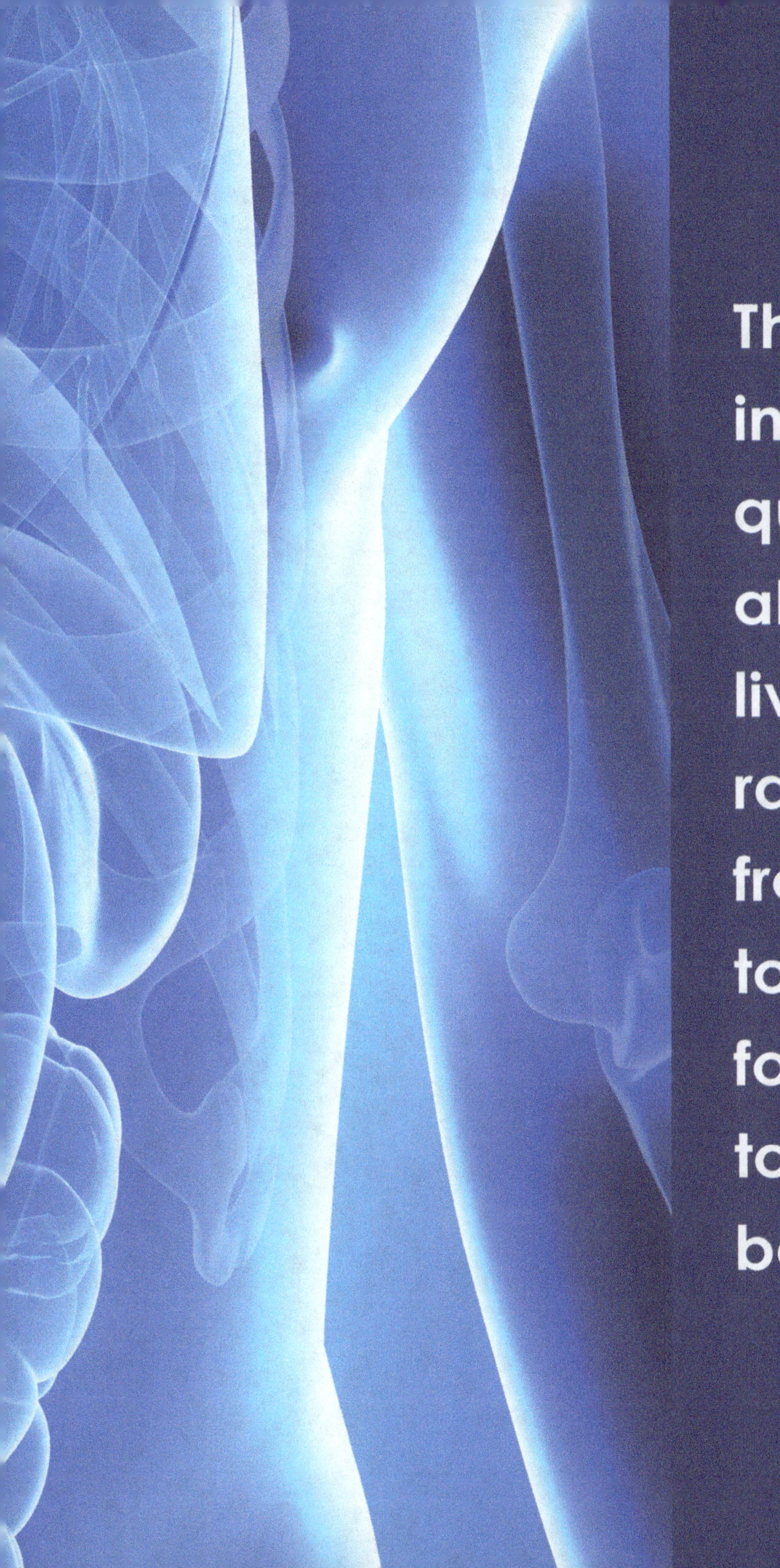

The liver is located in the upper right quadrant of the abdomen. The liver has a wide range of functions, from helping us to break down food in digestion to ridding our bodies of toxins.

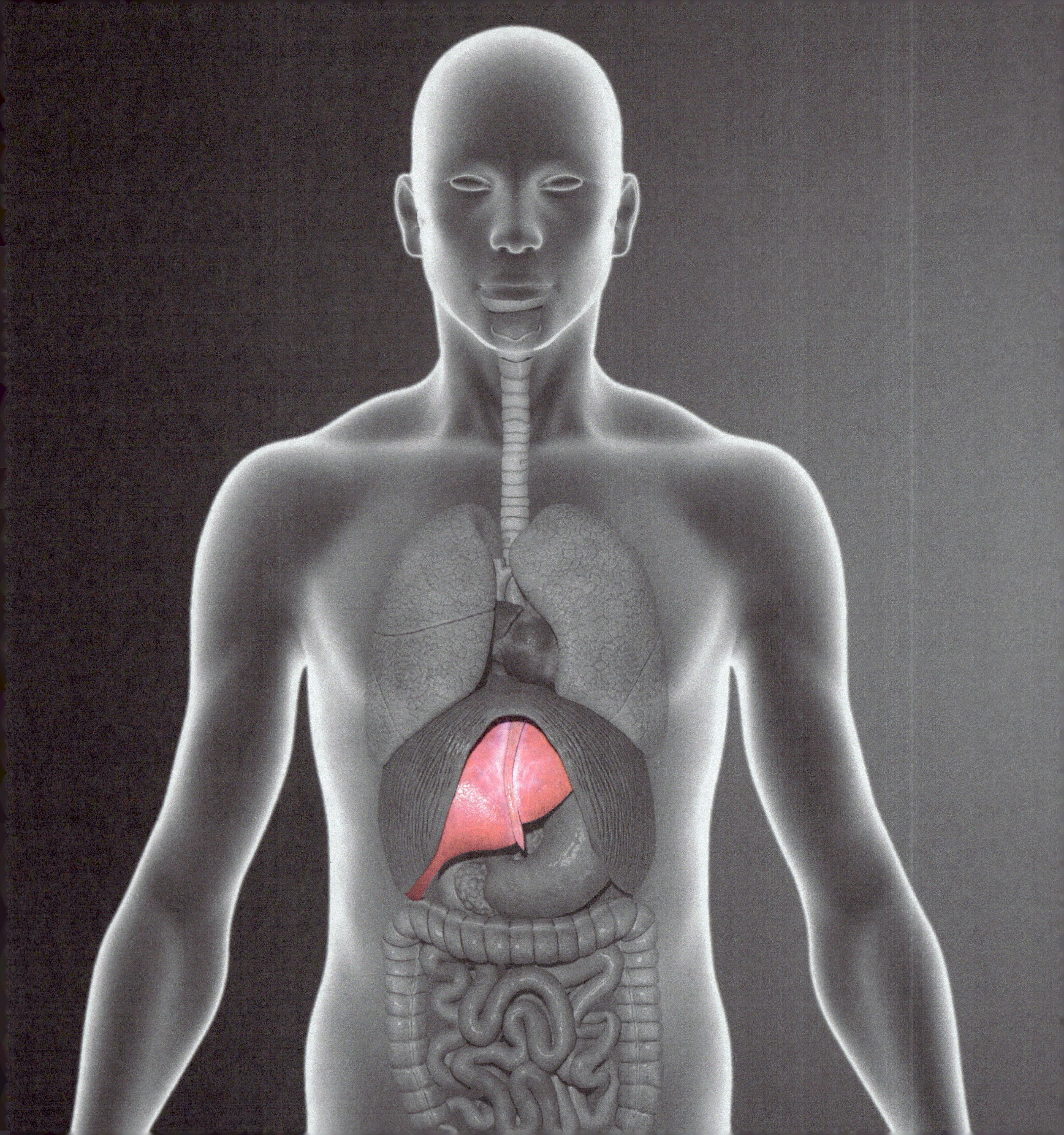

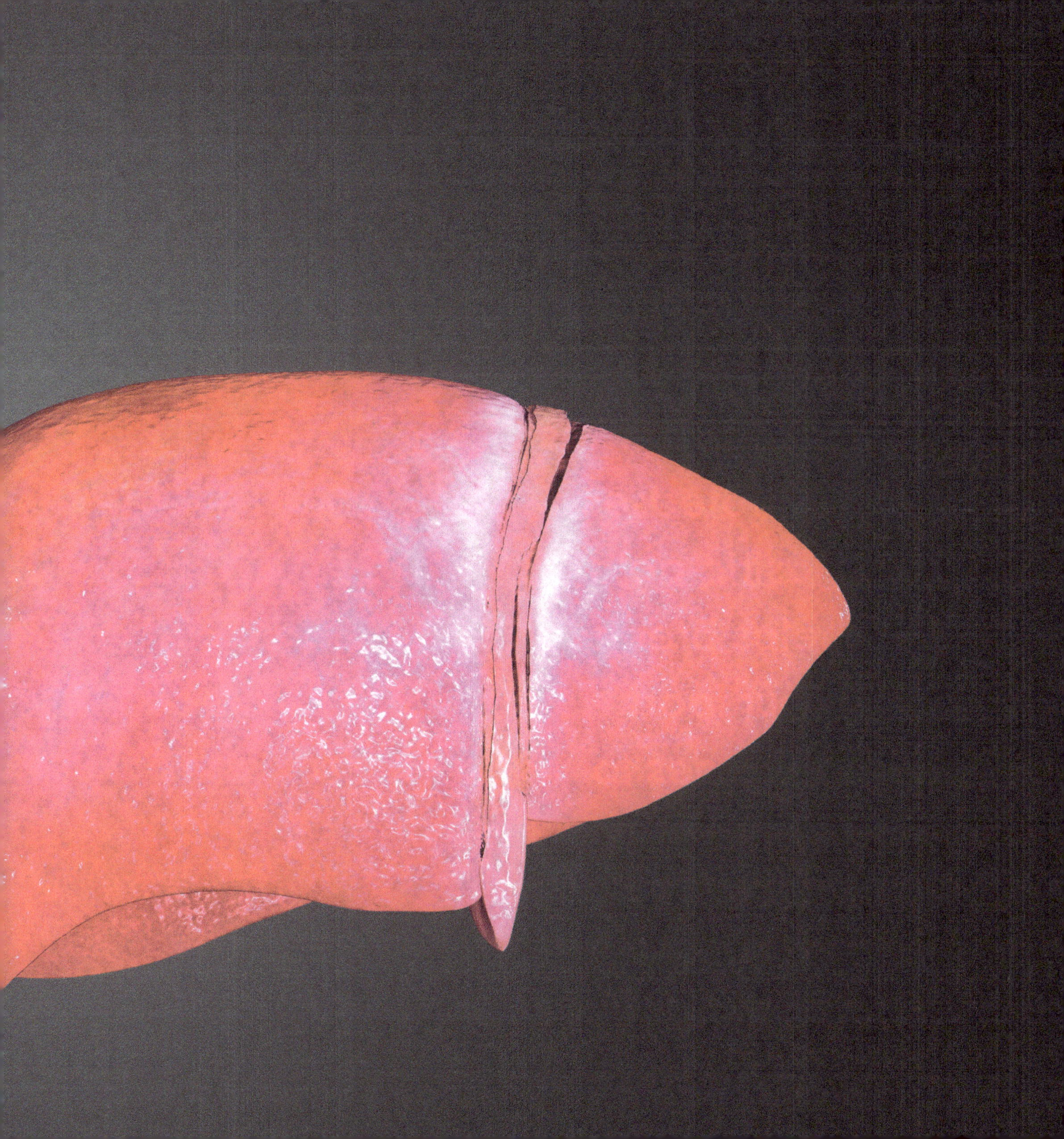

The stomach
secretes protein-
digesting enzymes
called proteases
and gastric acid
that helps break
down our food
before it goes to
the small intestine.

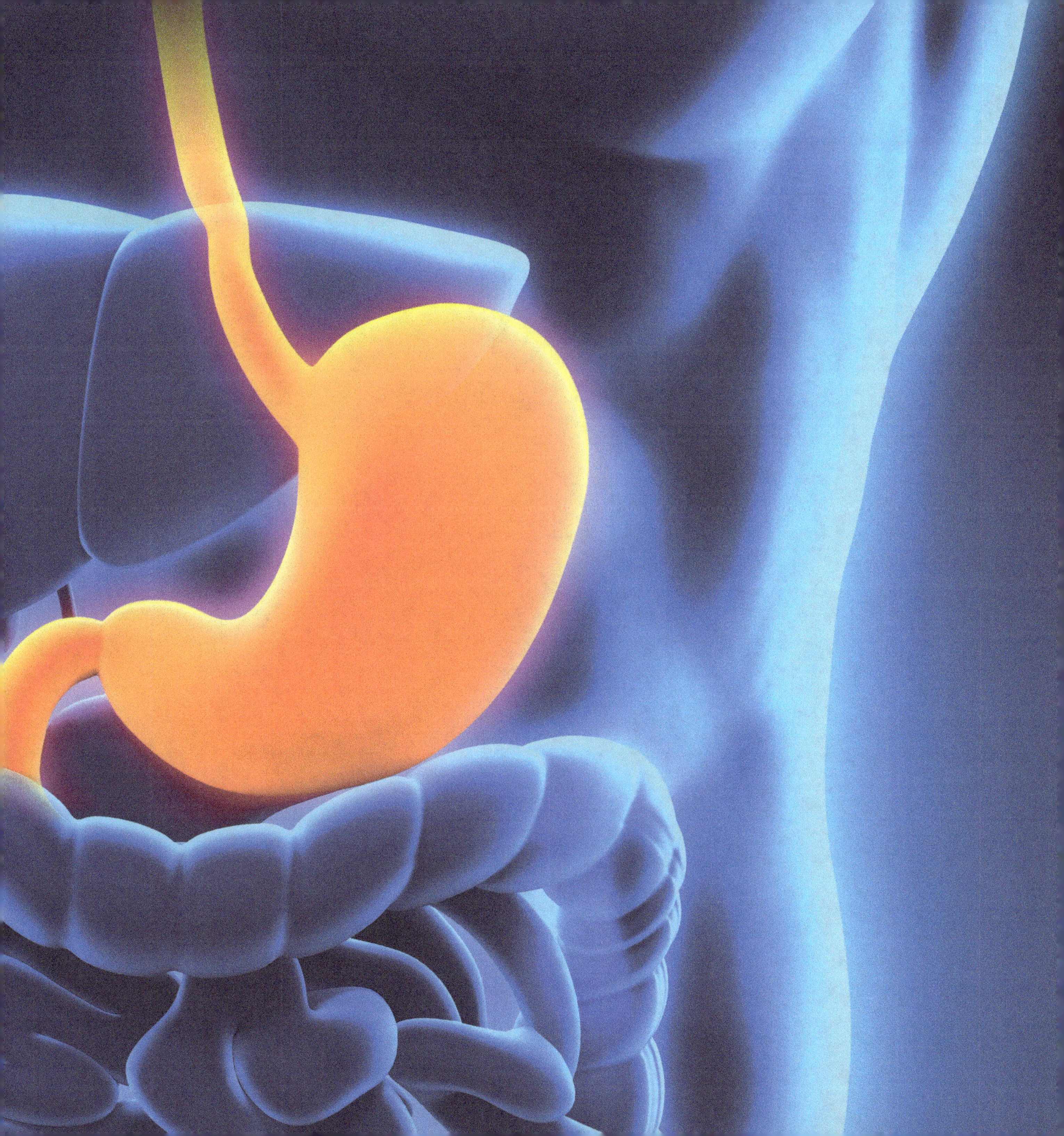

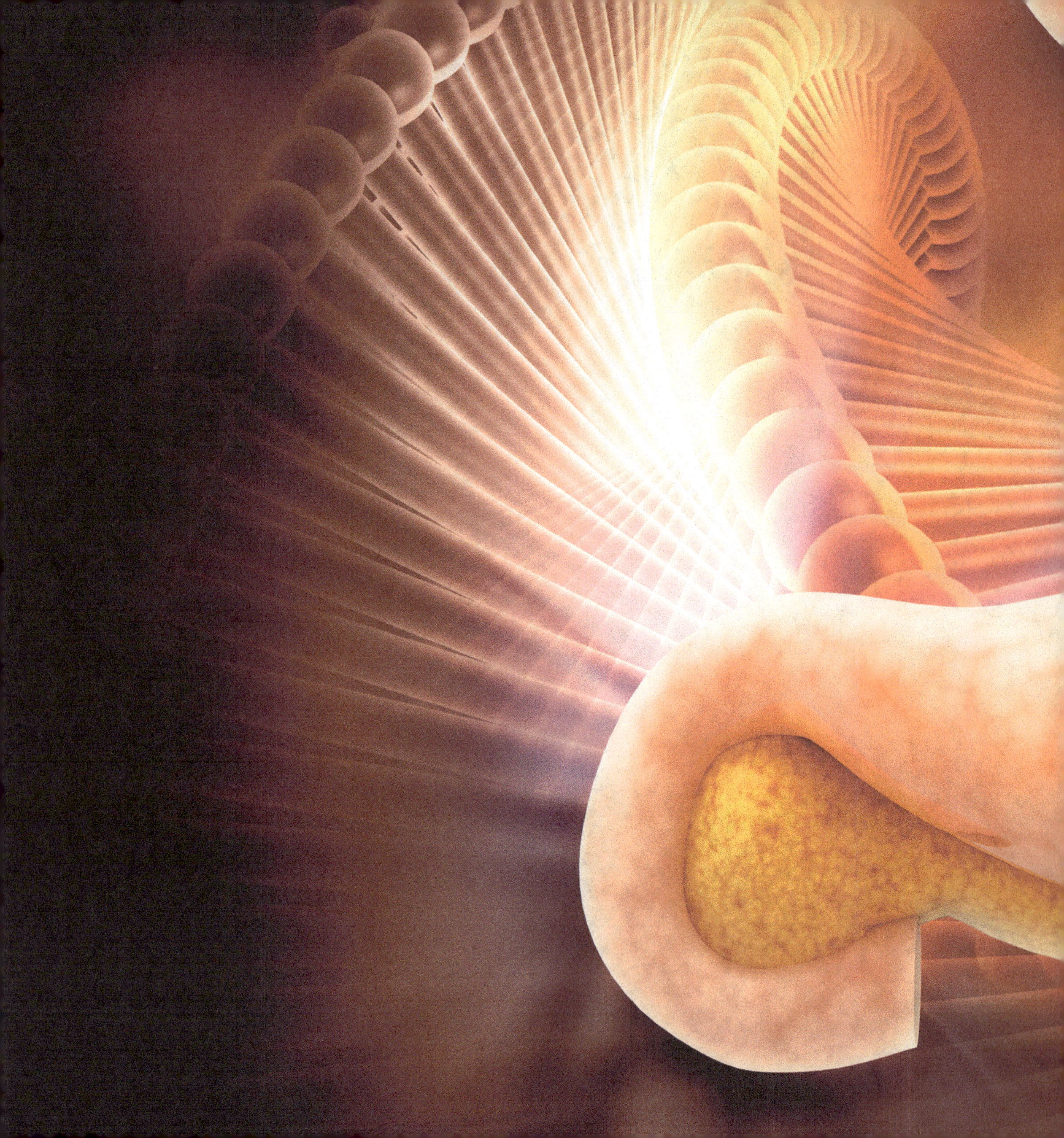

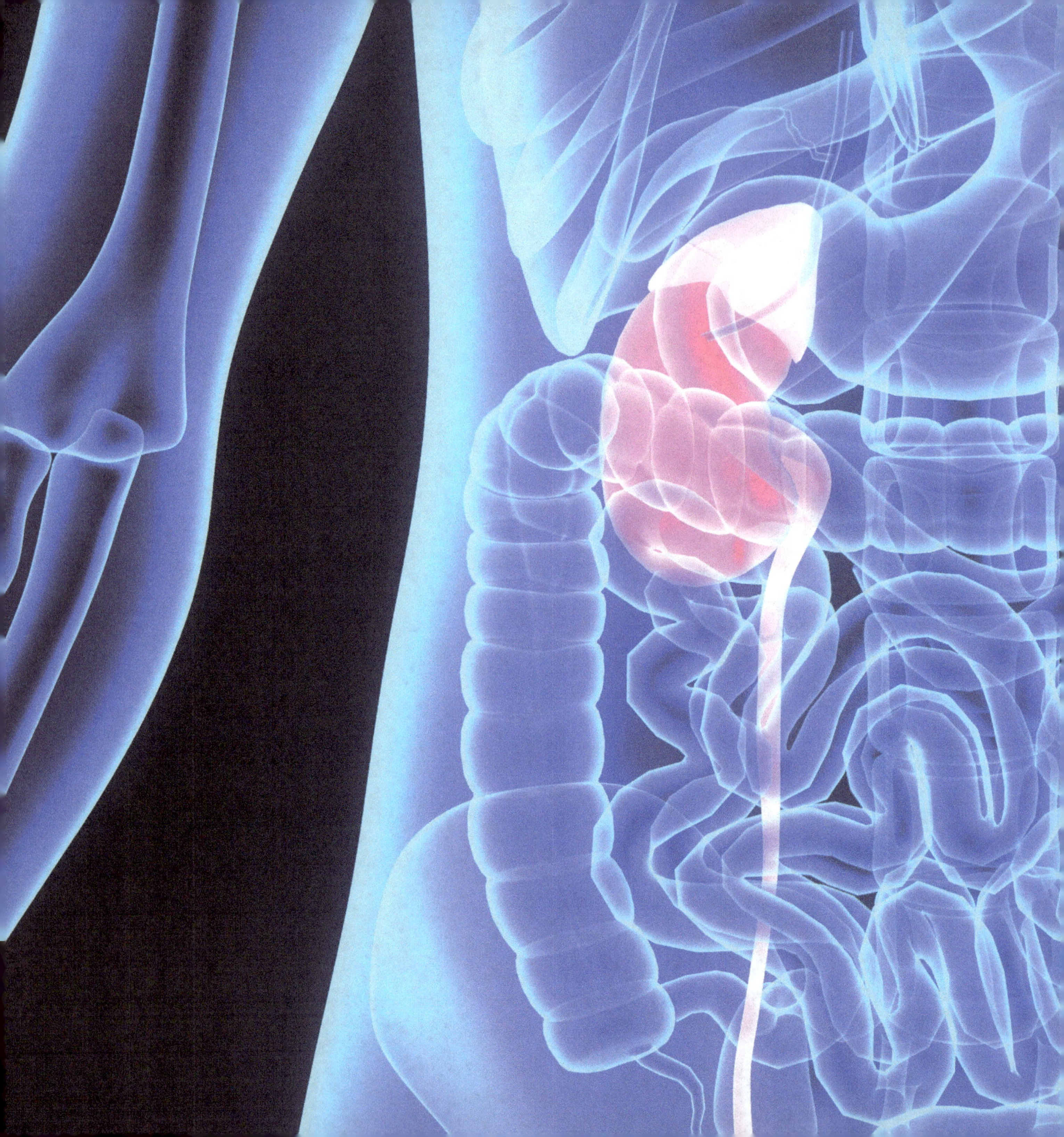

The kidneys
serve the body
as a natural filter
of the blood,
and remove
water-soluble
wastes which are
diverted to the
bladder. Without
our kidneys our
blood would
quickly become
poisoned.

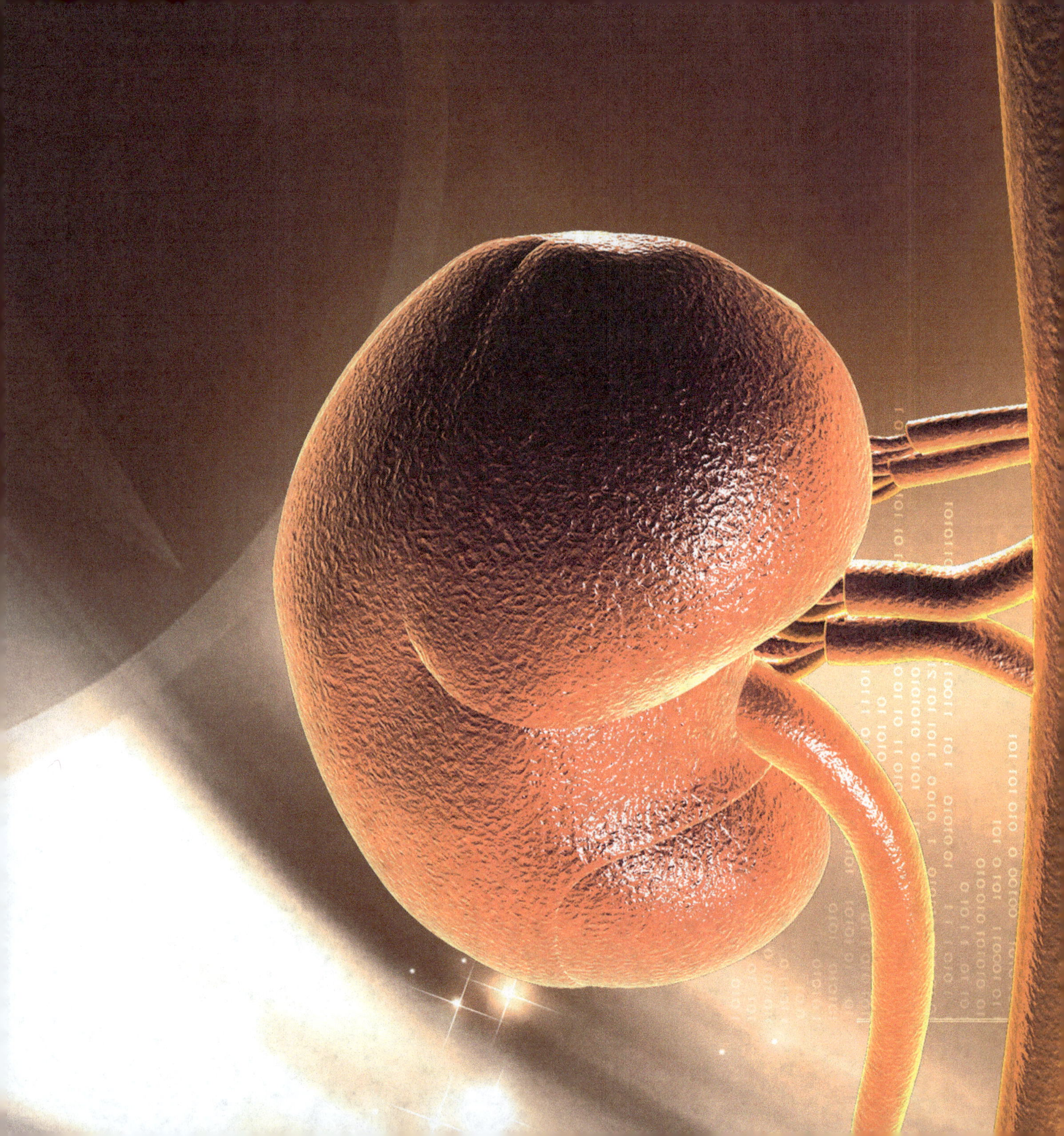

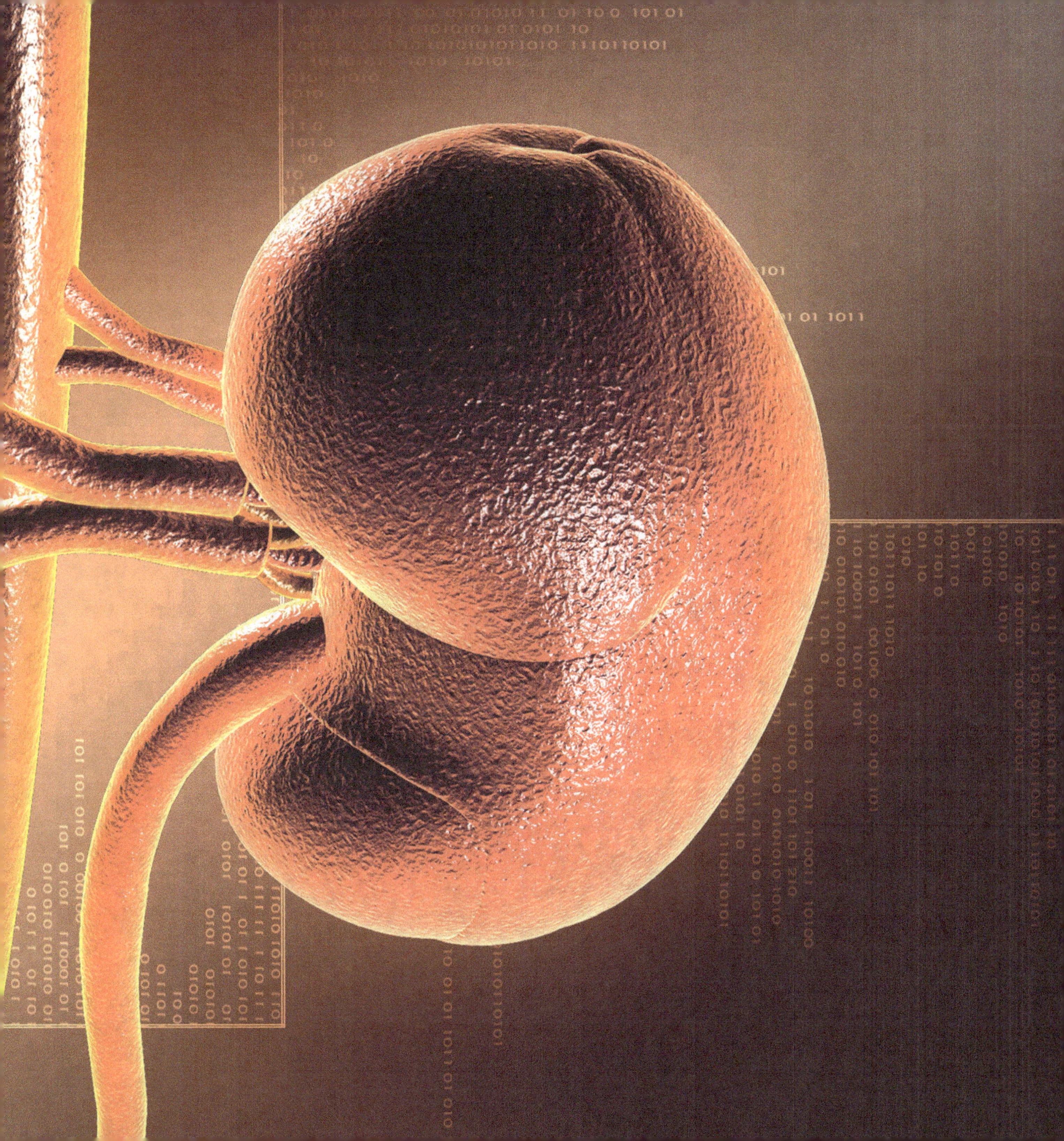

The heart is considered by many to be the center of life. The heart is a muscular organ which pumps blood through the blood vessels of the circulatory system.

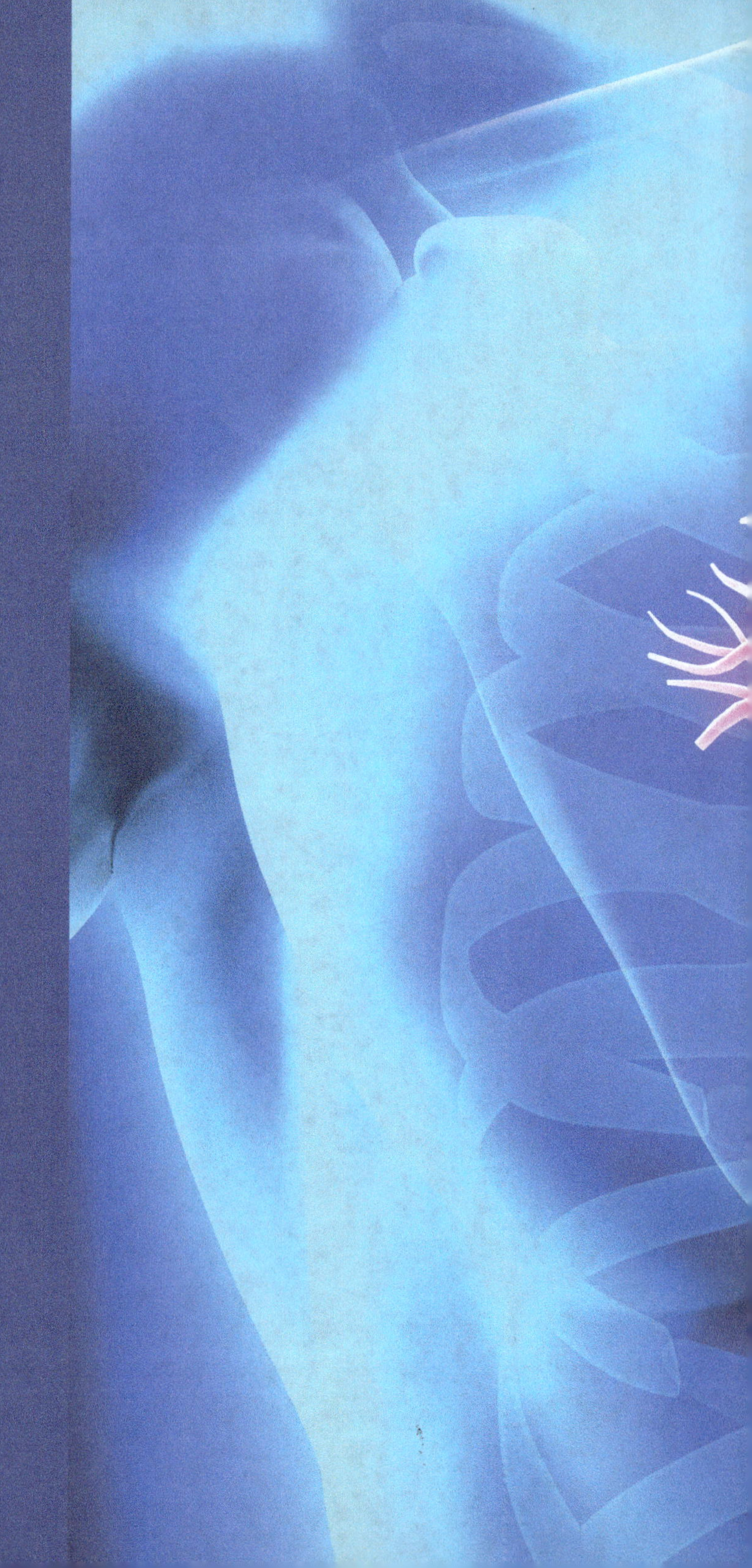

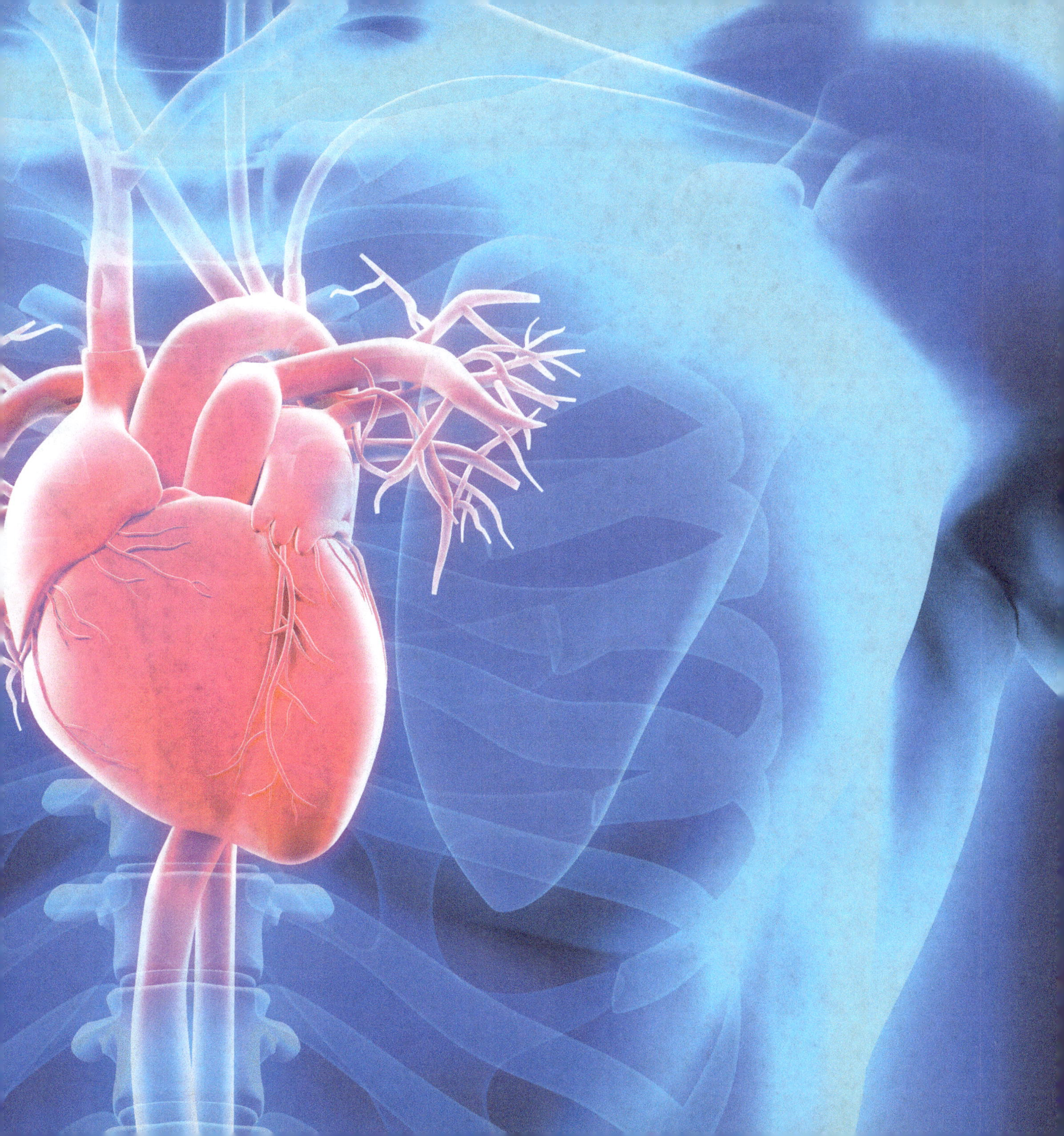

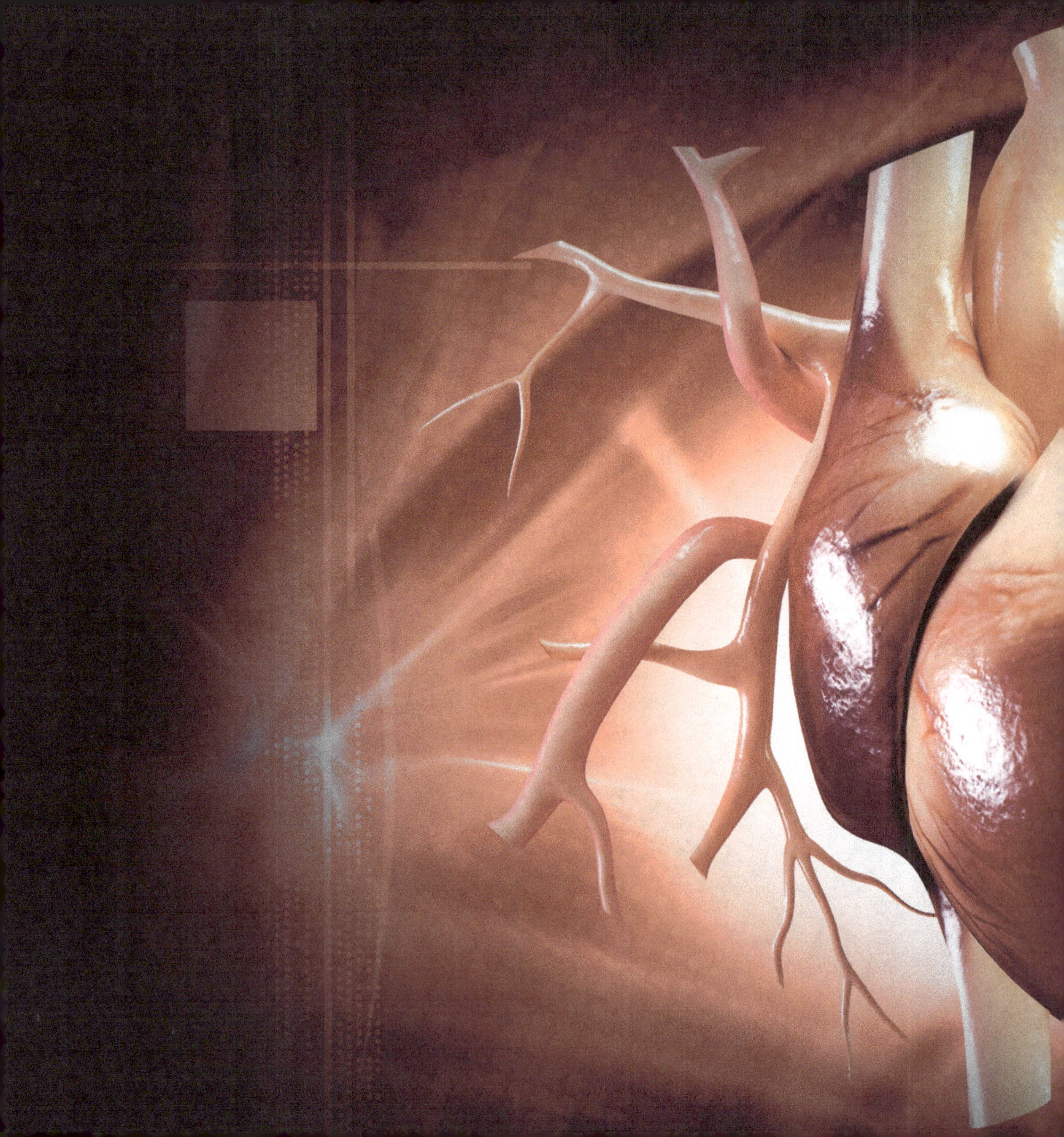

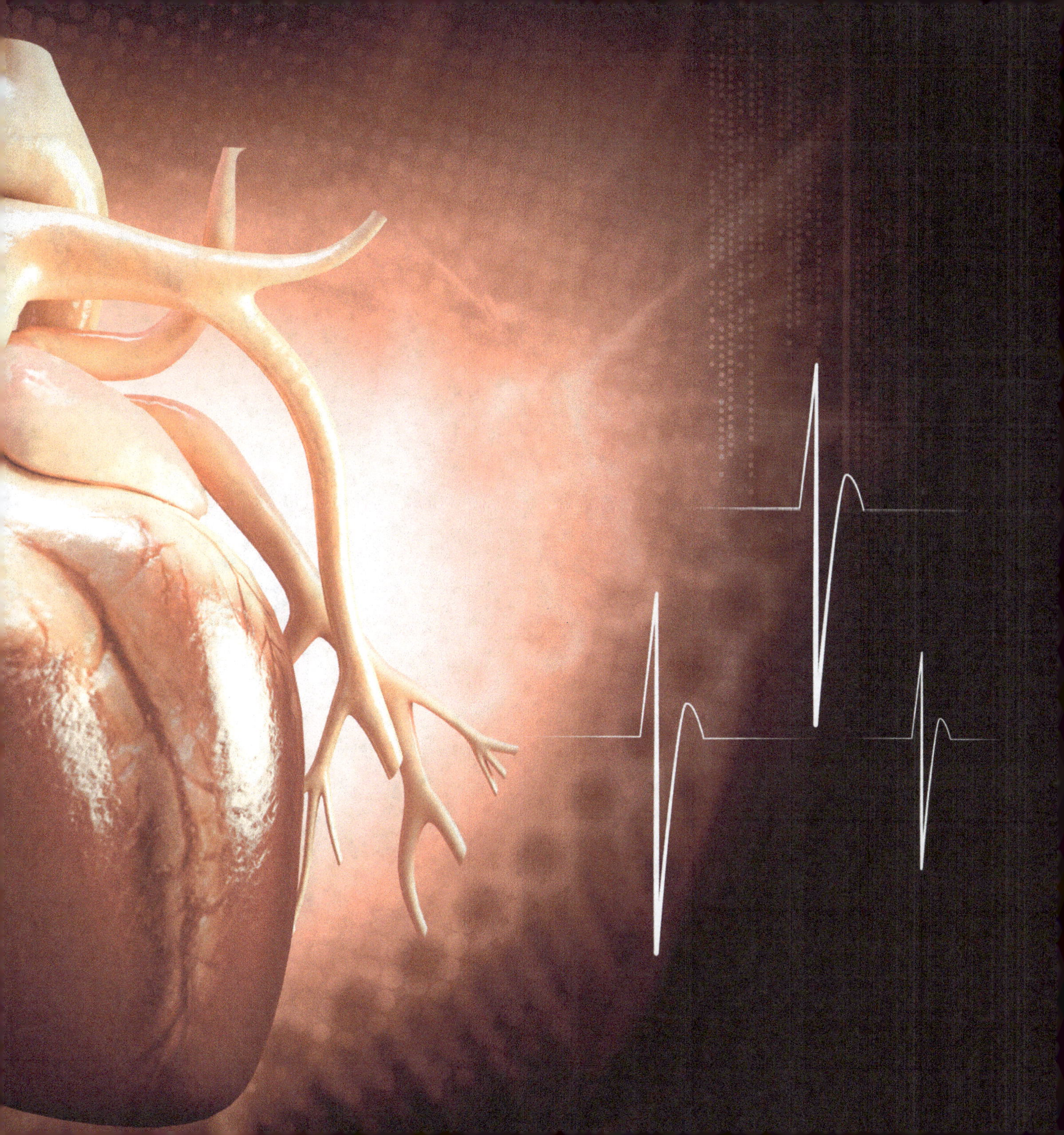

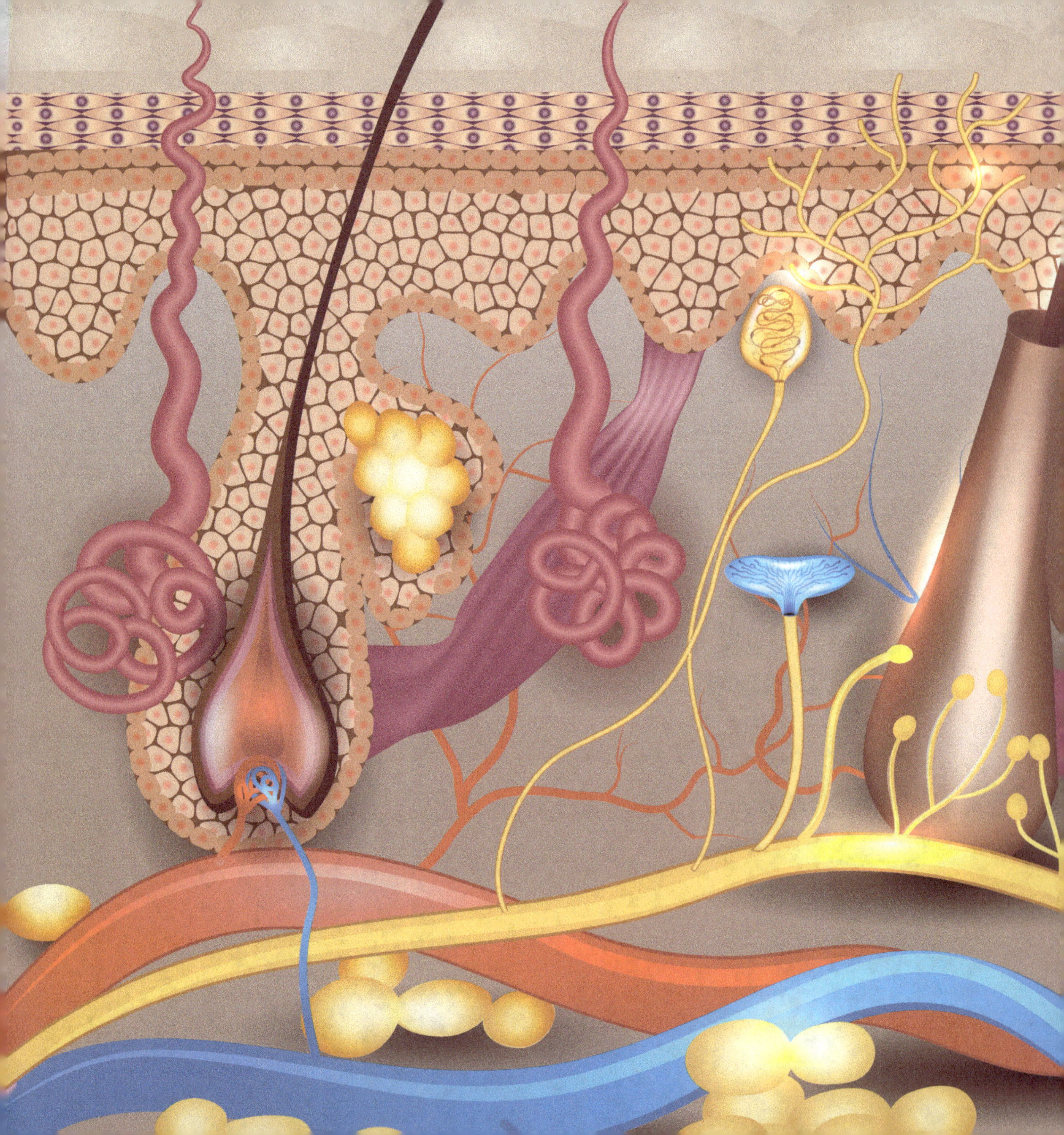

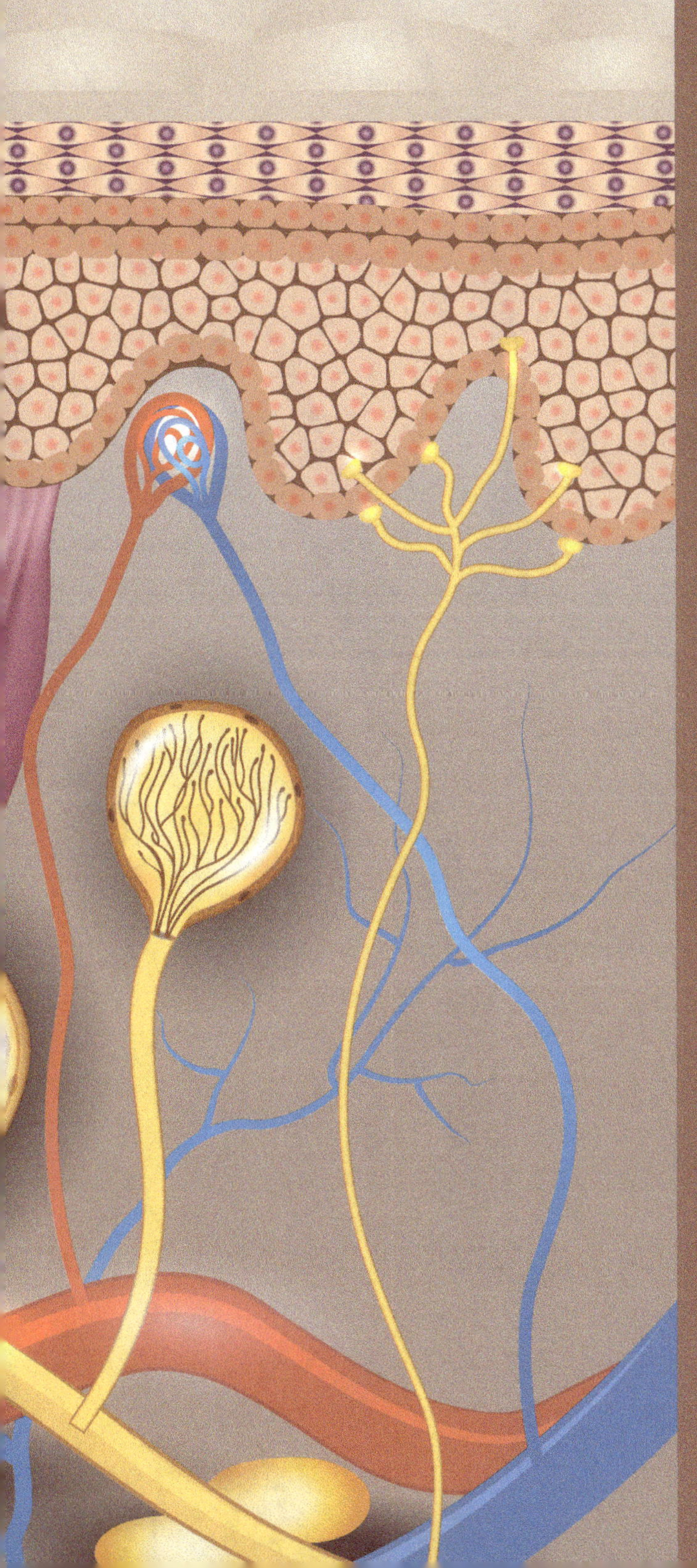

The skin is a major organ that covers our entire body. Skin is the human body's largest organ.